# Who Will Marry Maisie?

## A Traditional Tale

**Jane Langford**

**Illustrated by Nick Schon**

Maisie Rat wanted to marry Little Rat.
But Papa Rat said,
"You will marry the strongest one in the world!"

"Do I have to?" asked Maisie.
"Yes," said Papa Rat.
Maisie was so mad that
she jumped up and down.

Papa and Maisie went
to find the strongest one in the world.

“You will marry Sun,” said Papa.
“He is the strongest one in the world.”

So Papa and Maisie went to meet Sun.
"You are the strongest one in the world,"
said Papa.
"Will you marry my daughter?"

"No," said Sun.
"Cloud is stronger than me.
He is so strong that
he stops me from shining."

So Papa and Maisie went to meet Cloud.
"You are the strongest one in the world,"
said Papa Rat.
"Will you marry my daughter?"

"No," said Cloud.
"Wind is stronger than me.
He is so strong that
with one huff and one puff
he blows me away."

So Papa and Maisie went to meet Wind.
"You are the strongest one in the world,"
said Papa.
"Will you marry my daughter?"

"No," said Wind.
"Stone Man is stronger than me.
I huff and I puff all day,
but I can't blow him down."

So Papa and Maisie went to meet Stone Man.
"You are the strongest one in the world," said Papa.
"Will you marry my daughter?"

Stone Man looked very sad.
"No," he said.
"Little Rat is stronger than me.
He is digging tunnels under me.
Soon I will fall into the ground."

Papa and Maisie went to meet Little Rat.
"You are the strongest one in the world,"
said Papa.
"Will you marry my daughter?"

Little Rat looked at Maisie.
"Yes, I will!" said Little Rat.

Maisie was so happy
that she jumped up and down.